MW00611098

a little bump
in the earth

ALSO BY TYREE DAYE

Cardinal
River Hymns

a little bump in the earth

Tyree Daye

COPPER CANYON PRESS

PORT TOWNSEND, WASHINGTON

Copyright 2024 by Tyree Daye
All rights reserved
Printed in the United States of America

Cover art: Courtesy of Tyree Daye

Copper Canyon Press is in residence at Fort Worden State Park in Port Townsend, Washington, under the auspices of Centrum. Centrum is a gathering place for artists and creative thinkers from around the world, students of all ages and backgrounds, and audiences seeking extraordinary cultural enrichment.

LIBRARY OF CONGRESS CATALOGING-IN-PUBLICATION DATA
Names: Daye, Tyree, author.
Title: A little bump in the Earth / Tyree Daye.
Description: Port Townsend, Washington : Copper Canyon Press, 2024. |
    Summary: "A collection of poems by Tyree Daye"— Provided by publisher.
Identifiers: LCCN 2023042442 (print) | LCCN 2023042443 (ebook) |
    ISBN 9781556596889 (paperback) | ISBN 9781619322912 (epub)
Subjects: LCGFT: Poetry.
Classification: LCC PS3604.A9884 L58 2024 (print) |
    LCC PS3604.A9884 (ebook) | DDC 811/.6—dc23/eng/20231010
LC record available at https://lccn.loc.gov/2023042442
LC ebook record available at https://lccn.loc.gov/2023042443

9 8 7 6 5 4 3 2 FIRST PRINTING

COPPER CANYON PRESS

Post Office Box 271
Port Townsend, Washington 98368
www.coppercanyonpress.org

for my mama, Joyce Glover, who raised me into magic

for your continuous love and support, De Lissa Daye

for all the people, and the little town we made on the hill

Black subjectivity is not swallowed up by the ship itself. Rather, the ship, its crew, black subjects, the ocean and ports, make geography what it is, a location through which a moving technology can create differential and contextual histories. To return to Equiano, the slave ship is not simply a container hiding his displacement. It is a location through which he articulates hardship and human cruelty, in part mapping and giving new meaning to the vessel itself.

Katherine McKittrick, *Demonic Grounds: Black Women and the Cartographies of Struggle*

Contents

a little bump
in the earth

To the people of Nassau Street.
I wrote a book for you. It is not enough.

~~RENTAL AGREEMENT FOR YOUNGSVILLE COMMUNITY HOUSE~~

The undersigned agrees to bring every cousin   aunt   uncle   ghost   the
cursed   the great-greats   the elders   tell us stories of   so we recognize them   by
their shoes   and the way they use their one hand to hold the other   which of
course is the way we hold ours

The undersigned agrees to bring everyone from everywhere   our lives have
taken us   because we are here to celebrate   the birth of new children   the passing
of grades   graduations in ~~and in consideration of being allowed to rent~~ the
Youngsville Community House (herein-&-after referred to as the "Ritual House")
for the following date(s) It is ours now to the following terms and conditions: ~~The
undersigned agrees that he/she has received and read a copy of the Youngsville
Community House~~ We agree to nothing but the light & dirt   which is God

Rules: The undersigned agrees to abide by and ~~ensure that his/her guests abide by
said rules~~ tides

Initial by remembering your grandmama

3

~~The undersigned agrees that failure to abide by said rules may result in the entire party being asked to leave the House~~ No one will be asked to leave the Ritual House while our ~~his/her~~ function is still in progress/Or when it is over   stay some years   We have removed the clocks   so there is time   The undersigned ~~agrees to leave upon being asked and understands that his/her rental amount paid~~ up front will be forfeited ~~and that the security deposit will also be forfeited~~ in love

Initial by saying your grandmama's name

~~The undersigned will~~ assume all responsibility for: ~~any and all damages caused to~~ the Ritual House as a result ~~of his/her rental thereof, even if the damages exceed the amount of security deposit charged and paid for the rental.~~ of how many ways we've taught you how to cook fish

Bow and initial now

~~The undersigned understands that failure to follow all rules may result in not being able to rent the House~~ in the future   which is behind you ~~this includes damages and failure to~~ properly clean the House of old masters

Initial with your grandmama's eyes

~~The undersigned agrees to accept responsibility for and indemnify~~ the Town of Youngsville ~~for any and all claims for damages arising out of the use of the House pursuant to this rental agreement, unless said damages result directly and solely~~ from a preexisting unsafe condition will not be welcomed in the Ritual House ~~way exist.~~

Initial with your grandmama's courage

~~The undersigned agrees that~~   failure ~~to cancel the event in a timely manner, minimum of two weeks before the scheduled event(s),~~ will result in a loss ~~of deposit.~~

4

Initial child and be saved

~~Customer is liable for the pricing in effect on the day of rental according to the fee~~ ~~schedule in effect~~ on the day ~~of rental. Current Fee Schedule~~ of oxtails we can be found at ~~tinyurl.com/Youngsville-budget~~ our meeting spot   in the woods

Initial by drawing an outline of your face

~~The undersigned has read this agreement and understands the provisions~~ therefore This ~~agreement constitutes the Entire Agreement between parties regarding rental~~ ~~of the~~ House is ours

In the final days of the blue earth

Mailing Address	*My God we have nowhere to go but in.*
(Address to Mail Refund)	What do you have to give back(?)
Phone Number	Phones Off
Email	No Computer
Type of Event	We will be mostly bringing back the dead.

Instructions for cutting loose the Ritual House: (1) find the gutter like a snake in your yard & cut it open; (2) when you get to the end, find its friend and keep the cutting coming; (3) hum while you're wounding/hum for the wounded; (4) after enough vibrating, hold the spine in one hand & the house in the other.

Do-si-do

In purple rain boots   E'vel danced out of the town's song—
she put one little foot down
then picked her grandmama's knee up again   quickly
slamming down the granddaddy one

thunder   someone turned around and offered

E'vel made it thunder four times in a row
before Jo'Anne began to stop the music
but the storm's rhythm was caught
& cornered inside us
older than the hill's first field of cucumbers

We heard a song made of a language we had
no home for in our mouths
we knew the chords were saying   *I love you all*
like when our grandmamas speak
from the grave of a known & unknown calling

the dead knew this song

Uncle Gig's ghost finally left the no-account chickens alone
& added a low ghost hum
to our Black road song

the song sounded like syrup
sorrow a Sunday when nobody died
of syrup like blood or sorrow eyes

a Sunday when nobody went to the other side

the song played through our living
until they came out
of their frog-croaking screen doors

they put the song's sorrowfulness in a bigger bowl
they made the syrup sweeter & the Sunday longer
syrupupupup *sorrow*
a Sunday when nobody died for years
the song spiraled on
speaking to each person in this train-tracked-over town
a little verse & hook of them

The Tomato Women heard an anthem rising
from the sandy loam
they grew their tomatoes in
they never heard the soil speak such words
before   they were hesitant
to put the dirt in a pot   to lift from the ground
what bounced like a house speaker
playing your daddy's song

when the sorrow got to the oldest people on the hill
they said the singing reminded them of hungrier times
their mamas' half-asleep songs sung to them
as navy bean–eating children

Jo'Anne knew like mamas sometimes know
what the song is made of
and how a harmony got in her babies' legs
E'vel was Jimmy's through & through
& all that carrying around Jimmy do with the dead now
gave their brown child gifts

& God had a sweet plan for her E'vel
that made her worry
and made her hands move away
a bit of sky

The Matter of Things

I'm telling you the plain truth. You would think
a town with this many poor folks—
peeling backyard potatoes was bitter-bathed,

but when I got off the pencil-colored bus
my mama was waiting there laughing with the other mamas,
with a thick piece of maple at her hip

for any carolina dog between here
and where she'd covered my room
with a thousand plastic stars.

We are citizens of their upstairs laughter
& their   *I ain't cryin'* tears
carried to two jobs—

cleaning faraway office buildings
four nights a week.
My house like everyone's had a table

to sit down some troubles.
When the emptiness chose us
we dumped out lonely in the river

like bad sugar wine,
or held each other near the wicker basket with the fish
who like us learned to embrace

in death. You would think we desired
to keel over in the dirt
around our slapboard houses

but we greased our legs
& went out into our yards   made them
hot pink, purple & beautiful.

We scrubbed our houses
like God was coming
to get a plate. You would think

we didn't have the time we bear
to plant flowers
and flour biscuits,

but every thumb here has had dough under nails
& is a green that sends our uncles into prayer.
We still gather near flames

because that's all our grandmamas had,
you would think
we couldn't kill a thing

but the deer ran into the wind-keeping woods,
so did the squirrels,
and the pitfall possums.

You would think
we made the reddest devil horns
when we heard the Lord's name out loud.

Begin with Me

I got up
off the ground
near some graves—I share
the last name with.

I begin,
with what I was handed:
a mama, a daddy I saw a few times,
because he hid
in the hues he knew.

My little brother full of love
like the corner store in heaven. I knew
his lying like I knew our daddy's lying:
same song, but a higher key.
My mama taught me to

ask my dead plenty of questions—
to let the moon touch me on the mouth,
to ring my black bell.

Mama's Poem

mamas of their mama's mama's God   mamas of cantaloupe & tomato meetings

timber cutting

         mamas
            who bound sticks

            with wool & called the bundling *a hand*

mama said to reach back with

         mama helped Cousin Tae

             scared of birds all their life

touch the wing of a robin   flying along the car

where mama was ready to flutter away from here   but mama stayed

mothball-laying mamas   killing every snake

in and out their yards

mamas of the land   that's been flattened out

            the black valley all the way gone

mamas who dance

       under the floodlights of a Friday night

       like pine needles do when burned

       by a child

       with their mama's lighter

mamas who sing what they could not name

              then pass the song on to you

mamas talking to dead husbands & nieces all night long

       turning over the hill

           looking for them

mamas who rivered us clean

       mamas who would & wouldn't

           strike their children

mamas who made themselves smooth as pond stones

       & circled their eyes

Friday Night on the Hill

       started with uncle's sugar wine
then a strawberry cake arrived in our aunt's hands
like a candy-stained-face child

someone out of luck and hungry
scrawled *that pain no more*
in the rust of all the Fords in town

the gentlewomen are not so gentle
when you ask them
to do your hair last minute
their fingers weighted
with a week so close to death
on a Friday night
we could get downright animal lonely

the only thing wounded in a field
I watched spirits entering a boardinghouse,
surrendering to a piece of plywood
made into a dance floor

the youngest of us wanted mostly
to be held for a mile
by our mamas
or an older favorite cousin
while they kick dust
to *Raspberry Beret*
we touch the coins of light
on our bodies
from Uncle Duck's disco ball

the chicken thawing
on the river-colored counter

have you ever seen Black folk shimmer
under floodlights & summer? We
                        are beautiful   you would think
                        we could grow out of the precious ground

there's a place on the hill we can go
that's hurt me in so many ways
but tonight   the hill loves me   I'm sure
as the dead do   it will roll

and love you
like a hill should

Jimmy Always Was

that dog in our neighborhood
to bite us through to the thighbone
then roll in the mess that rises from our bodies

so the year when God sent angels
disguised as hurricanes   flooding his powder-blue Mustang
we all slapped the scars on our legs

& laughed when we'd see Jimmy
on his hands and feet
headed to the corner store

when the sun was at its highest
his dog tongue on the side of his dog mouth
he would beg for water

eat your yard to clay
then make seven moons
before he fell asleep

God served Jimmy right
we said aloud
wished a flood on Jimmy too

Cantaloupe Stories

Strapped us in her blues,
in her blue Toyota
& we rolled down the hill   never hitting the gas.

       My mama got us to see Cousin Steve with the wind,

while he was in prison. I called him uncle
because I was a boy & he was much older than me, and often told stories
that started with *remember,* which I still think is wise.

They sat him in a coin-shaped field
of dust—not even like you keep cattle, purple lizards hurtled through
what grass there was.

At a splinter-giving picnic table the color of a ship's lower deck
we sat with him carrying the town in our pockets, news
of who was new to the hill,
who went through Ms. Shirley's temple
and was on the other side.

My mama gives us cantaloupe she brought
in her blue off-brand Tupperware bowl
like we did at family reunions.

As us kids tried not to ask the questions
we were told not to ask.

I saw my mama bury a twenty-dollar bill
under the table
then get back to missing him. Beneath the sun
tethered to every family there.
Making our visits dangerous,

beneath these booted guards
like given-up angels on a stone wall.

We were my uncle Steve's tendrils   I know that now.

He heard our stories as trills.

Cornrows

when grandmama died

      she had a head full of pressed hair

by now it must've grown around her

            like a canoe

         even dead   she's found a way home

her hair fills our rooms

         replaces the sheets on our beds

    I run my fingers through

             parting her scalp

tucking the hair at my shoulders

          where I can sleep

    my hair touches the middle of my back

    I make a home from my hands I press my face into

         my living uncles called me sissy

         my sins braided into my glory

         my hair dreaming

         it's as long as any field in Franklin County

Dream Book

Clams for mama's teeth again

I think it's because we by the sea people

a big bird making a fist in the sky was the moon

mama made her way through water

Geophagia

Our mama ate clay & lived

    to be one hundred and three

    is what Betty would say

when people in town touched their fingers to their chins
and told her they saw Vikki by the river

red all round her mouth

then Betty would simply walk away
'cause she will cuss about her sister
and she'd given up cussing years ago

Vikki was mama through and through
ate clay and sand like her
talked to the living like they talked to the dead
sweet as a heavy-handed
                              pie-maker

she knew the truth
was Vikki scared
the Bible songs out most of us
how she didn't clap on two & four
but on the *and*s
which made us go outside in the rain
& turn our feet side to side
like windshield wipers

if they let Vikki explain
Betty knew exactly what she would say

I was being eaten up
so I found some red clay
to clean myself
I needed cleaning   Betty

most of us do have dirt on the insides of us
                                                  not of the blue earth

  I was with the earthworms who saw everything
                          though their eyes are like mama's used to be

like mama they sensed the light   I was standing in
                                              a line of earth eaters

        old enough to be grandmama
        dreaming   I saw mama way back in the thick sleeping weeds
            with her mouth painted
        in mud the earthworms gathered their bodies into shapes
            a language I spoke
                    only with my thumb and pointer finger

Betty   I was full of the earth I pinched

                        then poured mama over me

Happy Birthday to Ya

Miss Lue, we share the same birthday as you know. I've always been a child

who needed to state things—

when it rained, I pointed out our thin windows

      & said   *mama it's raining.*

Miss Lue, I am sitting here remembering rain

and you filled my mind.

         And your little dog named Peach. Who believed

his little legs were oceans,

when they were barely rivers any of us knew the names of.

& when anyone got near your porch

Peach flooded the yard

         and how you called the oceans back.

I cannot look at your obituary

without feeling small teeth *round* my ankles.

I am a coward near the dead.

So I did not go to your funeral.

But I want to say Happy Birthday to Ya. Today,

I wanted to see your ghost in the window of your old brick house as I drove by.

I know someone in our hand-raised-to-Jesus town

would say that's of the devil,

        but God knows my broken heart.

'tween my gone people & me

grandmama was cousins with the blue earth
                her speaking full of ravens' calls
                her hurt was a spindle to her love

the valley full of the best bones
her son had around his heart

          I've mistaken all his folded baseball caps
for one-winged parrots

grandmama   does your son stand up in me?
or am I standing up in him?
                            I want both to be

tell me   all the ways I'm dying
    all the ways *I'm coming to see y'all*

what's rounder than death? is it the moon
a carolina dog sees sleeping
on your grave tonight? I wield my trust only to you

I carry a fear for the living
like a drunk uncle through a tobacco field
shushing by swaying

I'm a pallet on the floor for you
my mama made me
near the kerosene heater

in the morning go out and be
your best boneless self or stay in your house-

dress   I made a mercy with
all the flowers the dead held

—dropping them as they walked
in the middle of the street   I woke up

beside my grandmama writing
five hundred years in—to this American experiment

trauma made our mamas
                                    turn a thousand
made our daddies dead

Jimmy as the Dog He Always Was

you can die twice messin' with me

& your mama has no money

to bury you again

after i dig you up

no wild wind's weepin' will make you

into the risin' of the moon

your body   my robbery

your shames wanted   in my mouth

human   ham

i had a daughter

now i only have desires

you can see them both in my eyes

forget what you've been told

about dogs & daddies & our protectin'

Jimmy is howlin'

Jimmy has an ancient blood thirst

& you have the kindest

i mean gentlest   bones

Angels Come Down from Heaven

angels fell asleep in mama's pantry
& woke up wings stained
                            black with molasses

         so they had to spend a few days with us
on the ground letting cane melt
in the sun they'd chant

                    a Valerie June song
wings strumming the side of our house
like a guitar

                    they hung out mostly in front of the corner store
                    with bottle-passing old men
                    then kissed their faces while they slept

one angel held your uncle down
while the other scrubbed him clean
the night before he died

                    or they threw sand
                    in somebody's face & sent them to hell
                    angels smug as birdless snakes

an angel would witness a child
wield their will so wholly
the wound would lose its mind & steal a lamb
or any soft white animal

                    just to leave it dead
                    in someone's yard
                    like a cloud pulled down

an angel like a storm
come smiling down the road   and we'd run inside hollering *mercy*
the angel calling back   *mercy be*

The Lord's Corner

I would drop to my knees for the littlest things

mind filled with a light returning

from aluminum-foil crosses hanging on a porch

I was made to believe so hard

that I was going to die

My family said I wore bells on my ankles

                         I learned an ancient dance

Then the light like the deer

leaped off   into time

& once   because my cousins called my body a soft thing

because so desperately they said they wanted to kill

the woman I hid inside me

dared as they often did with their hands

to let my eyes wonder

where the thickest shine sat

we heard the last child had their mind stolen

the circles of their iris turned to coal

when they looked directly at the Lord's house

I'm trying find where I feel most at home

I believe it's inside me

Town Day on the Hill

I mentioned there was a song   *yes?* I mentioned the thunder?
how we memorized names by their rattle on the end?

                    did you hear how that song sang itself
                    up under blankets   into dreams?

so every year we fill our street

                              crooked as Aunt Coo's factory fingers
could you hear them shouting

                    beets berries carrots plums?
                    did you see the white folks coming & wanting
to take more than grandmama's peach preserves home?

          I'll never show you where we hid the children
we kept them in eyesight
                    like tears
                              sleeping on the face of a round-cheeked baby
everyone's swept-dirt yard was free of anything angels demanded
                              as we watched for snakes
                                        the color of wood ash
or fresh dark
          & how about the dogwoods?
          did I tell you why we brought them in from the wild?
          did I tell you what we were trying to remember?
                              they carried a hint of hawk
                              a smell more like a tongue

if you need to rest
rest under the fruit tree dropping pecans
                    somebody will come by to pie them

the crust alone will bring the people whose love is thicker than schoolbooks together

whether poor sick or scared   if you remember our uncle's lessons
and pray over the pie   you'll remember our aunt's
and dance

a little museum in the herein-&-after

What form can express the loss of something you never knew but knew existed? Lands you never knew? People?

Victoria Chang, *Dear Memory: Letters on Writing, Silence, and Grief*

An asterisk (*) identifies family research in "a little museum in the herein-&-after" done by Cousin Lisa D. Hayes.

Mingo Jeffreys and family in the 1870 census

Great-Great-Grandmama Ailsey, her husband
Great-Great-Granddaddy Mingo, and their son
Great-Great-Uncle Romulus were enslaved by
North Carolina senator William A. Jeffreys. After
William A. Jeffreys died young from typhoid fever,
Grandmama Ailsey was sold to Captain W. Harris,
Grandaddy Mingo was sold to W.F. Green, and
Uncle Romulus was given to Siddie P. Jeffreys. By
1870, the family had found each other and was
back together.

Carrie   *&*

Charlie

in the gar-den

(*clap*)

Carrie   *&*   *Charlie*

in the hill

Carrie & Charlie

in the gar-den

(*clap*)

Carrie & Charlie

in the hill

Carrie & Charlie   in the den

(*stomp*)

Great-Grandmama Carrie Debnam (*clap*) married
Great-Granddaddy Charlie Glover (*stomp*) on
December 27, 1922.

Use the circled letters to create a word that describes the relationship between a coral reef and a large ship. _ _ _.

Nature Poem

mushroom   bird   butterfly
me   mama   chair
paper baked to sun
a word inside us
never found

James Otis Debnam's WWI draft registration card

Family, place your questions for Great-Grandaddy Charlie here:

_____ ?

_____ ?

_____ ?

_____ ?

_____ ?

_____ ?

FORM APPROVED
Budget Bureau No. 33–R012–42

REGISTRATION CARD (Men born on or after July 1, 1924, and on or before December 31, 1924)
(Also for the registration of men as they reach the 18th anniversary of the date of their birth on or after January 1, 1943.)

SERIAL NUMBER	1. NAME (Print)			ORDER NUMBER
W 477	James (First)	NMN (Middle)	Glover (Last)	12743

2. PLACE OF RESIDENCE (Print)

Youngsville — Franklin — N.C.

(Number and street)   (Town, township, village, or city)   (County)   (State)

[THE PLACE OF RESIDENCE GIVEN ON LINE 2 ABOVE WILL DETERMINE LOCAL BOARD
JURISDICTION; LINE 2 OF REGISTRATION CERTIFICATE WILL BE IDENTICAL]

3. MAILING ADDRESS

(Mailing address if other than place indicated on line 2. If same, insert word same)

4. TELEPHONE	5. AGE IN YEARS 18	6. PLACE OF BIRTH FRANKLIN
(Exchange) (Number)	DATE OF BIRTH FEBY 2 1926 (Mo.) (Day) (Yr.)	(Town or county) N.C. (State or country)

7. NAME AND ADDRESS OF PERSON WHO WILL ALWAYS KNOW YOUR ADDRESS

MR I N Alford Rt 1 Youngsville N.C.

8. EMPLOYER'S NAME AND ADDRESS

CHARLIE GLOVER Rt 1 Youngsville N.C

9. PLACE OF EMPLOYMENT OR BUSINESS

Farmer

(Number and street or R. F. D. number)   (Town)   (County)   (State)

I AFFIRM THAT I HAVE VERIFIED ABOVE ANSWERS AND THAT THEY ARE TRUE.

DSS Form 1 (Rev. 11–16–42)   c16—21630–4   (OVER)   James Glover
(Registrant's signature)

James Glover's WWII draft registration card

My family has been in Youngsville, North Carolina, for over two hundred years. I would go to Youngsville, my sacred place, if the world were ending. My foundation as a person and artist happened there. It is my wounding ground. Youngsville was made by enslaved people, who shaped and constructed its lands and buildings. In establishing "a little museum in the herein-&-after," we discovered that the present is a catalyst for the past, and the past propels toward the future. Space existed as a mechanism to contort time. A space where we could bring back the dead, and the dead are brought back. When we say we remember, that memory is happening. We are there. We are moved. Space became the vehicle where we could see the people we were missing again. Poetry and all art allow for this, a timelessness that creates a path that resists the linear.

Angel Fish Arrival

gather dried flowers
trick an angel for its wings
catch a fish
see three ghosts
wait for someone to fish openly
on a Sunday the angel will arrive
in the newest way to say water

Family, place your questions for Great-Grandmama
Carrie here:

_____ ?

_____ ?

_____ ?

_____ ?

_____ ?

_____ ?

_____ ?

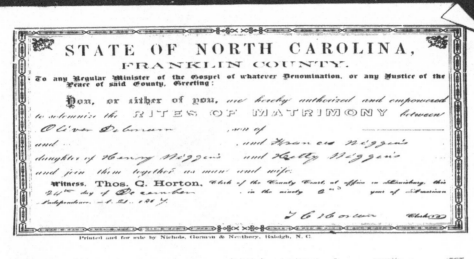

STATE OF NORTH CAROLINA,
FRANKLIN COUNTY.

*Oliver Debnam and Frances Wiggins's 1867
marriage certificate

Protect the Children

> when the first angel arrives
> tend to the flowers left behind
> use them to show the next angel
>
> when an angel arrives
> don't let the children go from your eyes
> the angel will get so close to them
> you expect it to take the child up in its arms
> forever to God
> and go

*Carrie Debnam as a child of James and Ailsey Debnam
in the 1910 census

on the stones

say their names
like they will walk from the next room
with their eyes kissed onto you
then bend the light
round their faces

the names on the stones

Charlie Glover (Uncle CG)

James Glover

Louise Perry

Carrie Eaton (Snook)

Samuel Turner (Turner)

Lela Mae Hayes (Monkey)

Willie Glover

Roosevelt McDonald Glover (Mac)

Charles Glover (Duck)

Uncle George Glover

Lillian Chamblee

Lillie Mae Glover (Lil)

Aunt Peggy Ann Butler

Aunt Barbara Ann Fant (Bug)

Reggie

David

Harold

Earl

Percy

Carrie

Joni

Kim

Aunt Serna

Aunt Lillian

Joseph (Uncle Boo Boo)

Lennel

Vickie

La Vern

Mark

Johnny

Mattie

Douglas

Chuck
Janice
Claude
Mrs. West (Butler)
Jeffery Muriel (Butler)

*"the names on the stones" is a list of family
members passed to the other side.*

exit here but take what you've felt with you

Proofreader

Between Duke & Elizabeth is Old Man Dallas,
all three were known as singers & gamblers
& cooked the meat right off the bone.

Near Old Man Dallas's left knee Mr. Brooks,
who carved miniature people out of branches
broken loose by wind & scared the children,
told them the little carvings had spirits
& Baby Claire swear she saw one move.

At the center Ms. Shirley, who was building a temple
in her backyard, she had one room of four,
on the door of that room read
bridge to the other side.

Vikki was known to see angels
in what old folks called the ether,
& was quoted saying the church's chimes
seemed to sing *oh baby, oh baby* & ended too soon.
The way *Fire and Desire* ends
& you wish there was a little more.

& there was Miss Bee, who became enchanted
with renaming things she thought had the wrong names.
She would go missing to be found in the wood
holding the velvet antlers of a doe saying *mama.*

I try to stay true to the pronunciation of names
like Buck, Miss Lue & Uncle CG when I go looking for them.

Mama keeps telling me when they call
I don't have to go, but I turn up like a weed
in the collards. I hold

my cell phone flashlight, a ghost lantern.
I steer my body through the dark churchyard,
slow as my mama drove her blue Toyota
pass the signs marking our children-playing street.

E'vel's Questions

what is my daddy suffering?
is my daddy's suffering: my what?
what is suffering my daddy?
suffering   is my daddy's daddy   is mines
suffering is my daddy's question
what dog is my daddy   what's suffering?
my   my   my suffering   what my daddy is

Uncle Pac's Blues

On supple nights, my light-skinned uncle Pac's nickname was *Chardonnay*.
He'd purchase some of Jo'Anne's homemade plum wine and replace all the blood he had
but what's *round his heart*.
Jo'Anne set up a store on her porch like her mama

in the summer selling Kool-Aid icy to the children, peach preserves
& for her daddy's plum wine my uncle Pac would sneak over,
forgetting his old grip on the necks of wine bottles,
his churchgoing and angel seeing.

After the sun fell, he'd start talking about the inner parts of thighs.
How soft the space is
between a woman's thumb & pointer finger, hands moving
like a russet pond. His tongue watering the inside of his jaws.

Back in the hill's day, he went by the nickname *Baby*
because he cried when he got drunk.
On these nights when what touched Uncle Pac went under
the toes, he had to follow

with a long corridor of water
in the morning. A dark
that when consumed you had to be already emptied.
He'd go to God to *let him begin again*.
A sanctified dark that touched him
when we saw nothing touching him

   & then we'd hear the making of wings.

Ms. Shirley Writes Us a Letter from the Other Side

I've known y'all
All your winemaking lives

My daddy cut his hands like your daddies
Cut their hands in those tobacco killing fields

You made me have to sit down
And write this heartbreaking thing

With a stinger on the end
I hereby proclaim the shame I have for you

Like Jimmy's hands have for him
In our Black town

We all have our shames
Shame shouldn't keep our brains shipside

Shame like walking on the sand
Knowing there's plastic underneath

But y'all built the condo of shame
You carry the diorama of shame

Making your daddy's hands bleeding
On your kitchen floor

Shame on you
After he knocked it off him

Shame bigger than the ghost of a bear
How dare you die when you come with me

To the other side
When the sun got an eye fixed on us

You milked shame until you cried shame
Into the dirt

Which you believed held the dead
& must be shameless

Jimmy on the loose   *Jimmy on the loose*   *Jimmy loose*   *Jimmy on the loose*

Jimmy loose   *Jimmy loose*   *get lost Jimmy loose* *Jimmy loose Jimmy on the loose*

off his chain & on the loose   *Jimmy on the way*   *on the loose*   *Jimmy on the loose* *Jimmy*

loose Jimmy loose *jimmied loose*   *his chain in half*   *Jimmy on the loose jimmied*

loose his chain *Jimmy on the way*   *chain in half*   *Jimmy on the loose*   *Jimmy loose*   *loose*

gone

We Ate Moon

My older cousin Ham held up a cabbage in the coming-on dark
like he was being born again, his body growing from the root. I couldn't help

but see a purple orb, a purple moon. A few night crows flew around
& rivers lifted out of their beds.

The true moon, astonished, hid behind one large cloud
away from the rest in the west. Ham spat on the ground

as he did often from years in a mill,
the inside of his chest a sawdust dance floor, a wooded way home.

He had mustard-stained eyes from putting his lips *round too many bottles.*
Tortured by land that ate crop, but this cabbage was the color of a jacaranda blooming

in his mother's yard. He was luscious & called out to God,
which I've never heard him do.

His luck had turned around, the soil opened up
like an oiled dresser drawer.

The evening was muggy
& I wanted to take a plunger to the sky.

We went into his clear-water kitchen, where he placed a cup in front of me
& a bottle of bucket gin.

In the cup a piece of ice blue as a hidden glacier.
The cabbage in a blood-drop pan with a little butter, & a little onion.

The Tomato Women's Meeting: The Washing of Hands

the water jug my grandmama clenched is undying the soil

when I feel the headaches coming I cup my hands

around her grave I make myself ready for rooting

Coo's way of gardening made her thumbs heavy as rocks used to hold an angel down

mama said Great-Uncle Uzzell paid the children fifty cents to scratch his head

I started growing these African Queens because I looked at Aunt Apple's swollen grip
                       & hoped her blood sugar levels would eventually go down

when the dead laugh it feels like somebody's tickling me

Jimmy killed cats as a hammer-carrying boy so now they follow him round

he's afraid they'll remember his terrible tossing

we cover our mouths & say Ailurophobia when we see him

the rain sounds like the clapping we did when Steve came home from prison

Dream Book

in uncle's suit we looked like him
you and I

        & we were not worried

at the beginning of our spiriting

Uncle Gig's Return

Uncle Gig stole a flashlight from Uncle Pac's shed

and cast himself on the side of my mama's porch

my mama said it was a gift

      like a rat in your house is a gift

I was told not to see him

but I was diamond-headed

he swelled in me like a river

because I was a drought expecting to happen

to witness it would have made you find your own uncle

on a bus looking for your grave

he was indistinguishable from a lizard

on your daddy's shoulder

Don't Say Love Just Signal

no one said hawk
we just looked at the sky
in the middle of a conversation

no one said when the melons were ripe
they were thumped and listened to
for a note we liked

a note like cane

no one had to tell the birds
to eat the seeds   we spat on the ground

no one had to tell the devil to make his rounds
in his many forms
with his many things

your mama my mama/my mama your mama
we never had to say so until now
because you feel more than far away
you feel gone

we'd all wake up one morning
and all the jacaranda trees were blooming
and no one needed to say a thing

we were having a good time & we were
so alive we lifted off the ground a bit
no one needed to call how we lived flying

& no one told us to come down
we could do this for   long time   love
like this   beside our grandmamas

watching Bob Ross on TV
make birds & bushes in her hushed living room

every summer a craft lesson
no one told us was happening

no one said   *child*   *write this down*

what the angels eat

as children we ate watermelons over trash bags
in my aunt's backyard
filled with so many black-&-blue-eyed crows
it stopped being a spell & they'd eat what fell between our fingers
& our skin stayed on

we'd get yelled at for spitting seeds at each other
       saliva thick with red
we made a war from the sweetest things
the flies made a mess of our dancing
the flies made a dance in our messes

our mamas thanked God it was not the blood feared

a watermelon's vine would wrap itself around you
if you fell asleep under them watching meteors
melons make magic under midnight moons

I once grew watermelons that flowers could sing
if I sat there singing
the way my aunts break out into song   I mean beautiful
like that the flowers would start moving

I'm so free I make a river on both sides of my mouth
a fruit full of kinship
it once grew wild and bitter
    in the Kalahari Desert
the grandmama of all the watermelons   the first water

my grandmamas share a bowl every Sunday
and drip the juice on the floor
but never stain a sole
the only fruit the dead can eat

Recipe

chicken has carried us along
away from death   I mean
a chicken can go a long way

                                into the summer
bones becoming a winter soup
my aunt would take a few of her barred Rocks
and my uncle would bring his Rhode Island Reds

a cousin unthawed three pounds of chicken feet the day before
from granddaddy's deep-blue freezer
green peppers chopped in half like a genie inside

& when you know how to get to the heart of your hunger
you can feed a whole town
when you like feet and necks in your rice

when mama taught you how to clean a knuckle
because she doesn't want your bones to show

you can do   ungodly things to animals

Sanctuary

I wasn't proud of my aim
at the bird I kept missing
& then finally shot through the head
even when the men around me stopped
looking down their guns
to glove my shoulders
to look into my cry-ready eyes
which is all I'd ever wanted them to do

Uncle Pac jumped from the ground
so I thanked God
he didn't become a bird
I'm sure we would have shot through him too

I want this story out of my mouth
my murdering of feathers
No   it was not an accident
where the pellet went   I went

the other birds chased their cousin's spirit
sobbing into the wind
I went to help them look   in the wood
I saw a see-through quill

       with my bright blue shame

The Death of Jimmy as the Dog He Always Was

when Jimmy's brown & wild was hit by the car

                                      all of him hollered & spun

a wild brown dog looked like a dust devil gathering wind

in an empty baseball field

a carolina dog in a town of factory workers & missing hands

with all the body could   Jimmy did a small brown dance

danced toward his death   not a dog no more

we wish we could forget but death was a view

a mountain full of snow

a trying mountain that almost made us forgive

but the dog in him would not lie down

a wild brown dog's blood is in our mouths   a carolina dog

& vultures at the roadside

an outfield full

of wild dancing was his dying

we got the look of his dying good in our hearts

of course the dog became the mountain

of course we wake to licking

Dream Book

my cousin Dalon shows up in all my dreams
I know it's because I love him

I was falling from a high place
but minutes before   Dalon told my mama
& she filled me with pine needles & pecan halves

my daddy was a famous writer
and he called me into his office   to read me his newest work

which was filled with snakes

snaking

~~~

when I'm a deep-brown snake getting my head cut off
            my uncles Boo Boo and George are alive
        & I can see them there standing over me

my heroes   my mouth slowly opening & closing   my killers
the shovel between my head & tail

~~~

when I am a dead snake I dream
of a field covered in dog bones & mice
& I am long & I am full

~~~ ~~~

they cut me in half & I am two green garden snakes
making love in my mama's brown grass

in other stories my uncles are at the corner store & they are alive
& I have no more snakes left in me

~~~ ~~~ ~~~ ~~~ ~~~ ~~~

my body can be whatever
they have picked up in their hands

I am a Budweiser 40

in a brown paper bag thick as moonlight they carry me
what am I when I'm this close
                        to the dead come back?

no rain will touch our squash for years if I look into their eyes
when they turn me up   they kiss my neck

& though I know their lives
I play along
I laugh a little
in dead men's arms

Controlled Burning/A Love Poem for the Hill

Because the valley was full of mirrors
holding themselves toward the light
                                    we turned our bodies to the side
                                            to face the controlled burning of that day

an abandoned slapboard house in our plain town
                    up in flames
                                & falling down
                                            inside itself

The town was a bathtub full of oranges
four children threw their arms up
in the chicken-feathered air

Before the house fell inward
        we felt the premonition of its falling
                                    and said our grandmamas' names

the unkempt gardenia eating the windows bent back into roots
            & lifted in the wind   the light turned into a sleeve of blades

a rain fell that was not enough & only ignited the glare

we kept our heads down   afraid we would change into luster
                        & would not return to our bodies   our devotion

A ghost because we have so many   shouted in the white firemen's ears
then turned   running toward the center of town   the brilliance
not aware of us and our dead   became twice itself
so we could not tell the distance between density & beauty
                a light we wanted to take our uncles' hammers to

Our legs if they were our legs   were trying to flee
to become unbound
the same soil under our mamas' nails
was under ours   so we wondered if we were unworthy
of the shining   the boards' splitting sounded like falling trees
the smell of a thousand burned-down forests making us
look at ourselves in the city water

mud all over what we thought was ours

untitled town poem: Confession

I looked & all the people had hands   even the ones I know did not

a velvet feeling & so I took the creased palms for my mama

wiping something from my mouth

everyone made homemade blowhorns out of old newspapers

& called out their own names

they wrote my name on rocks they threw into the river

the animal sound they made is still

making itself inside me

sometimes I touch them in the shower like glass

their stories had a lifetime of stories around them

I was a lowercase *i* inside them

so they said what they had to say

then they sharpened their front wings right in front of me

eventually the town was a town & not a tomb

they said my legs were growing branches

& they could hear others behind me when I walked

they put me in a parasol in the back

the walls could not take the wind

There's a Whole Lot of Love round Here

owls buried against the black roofs of houses

& axes lie against the back porch like lovers

a pocketbook full of bone readers told you why

    your great-aunt won't leave your baby alone

                with fire-makers   cucumber-cutters & rabbit-killers

cheap made so our houses flood
easily I cry my eyes empty

a whole soybean row of people waiting
for the first of the month made us a miracle making

dying in a minute wroth of hymns

           —————

some of them went blind from onions & cabbages molding
    in the dark some married under the natural arch
          pines and gums made in secret places

with no one watching
made their own laws and a looked-for life

some made the sweetest creams
and poured them over enormous cakes

a few folks were no-good and broomed out
into the dog-filled street

where they filled Budweiser 40s
with piss and sharpened chicken bones

some repeated everything
                    so someone could tell you
so you could tell yourself this
couldn't happen

& so some knew
they'd never die

Thank you

for visiting a little bump in the earth

Could you please take a moment and attempt to touch the farthest place you can see?

We'd love to hear about your hands

Come back soon   and remember the hill

Instructions for taking the hill with you: never die/take the wind we thought was ours in your arms/ with snakes we wake to blue shame/things animals can eat down/your shoulders filled with your beginning/when home is a little gone & must be made/calling back the bones   of everybody poured through water in Franklin County fields/our stories flood/like they should/our eyes a black bell/we hear in the sky.

Notes

"Begin with Me" borrows language from Lucille Clifton.

"'tween my gone people & me" is language borrowed from Nabila Lovelace.

"Nature Poem" uses language borrowed from *Daily Warm-Ups: Earth Science*, by Robert G. Hoehn.

"Don't Say Love Just Signal" is language borrowed from Al Young.

Acknowledgments

The American Poetry Review: "Angels Come Down from Heaven," "Begin with Me," "Cantaloupe Stories," "untitled town poem: Confession"

Boston Review: "Proofreader," "'tween my gone people & me"

Callaloo: "Cornrows"

Cero: "Mama's Poem"

The Georgia Review: "The Matter of Things," finalist for the Loraine Williams Poetry Prize

Harvard Review: "Friday Night on the Hill"

Los Angeles Review of Books: "We Ate Moon" (as "Ate Moon")

New England Review: "Don't Say Love Just Signal"

The New Yorker: "what the angels eat"

Southern Indiana Review: "Recipe," "The Tomato Women's Meeting: The Washing of Hands"

Washington Square Review: "snaking"

a little bump in the earth was conceived of while I was in a writing group hosted by my teachers Dorianne Laux and Joseph Millar and attended by poets Arielle Hebert, Matthew Wimberley, Erin Rose Coffin, Mariana Lin, Michael Montlack, and Leila Chatti. Thank you to the manuscript's early readers and listeners: Dorianne Laux, Joseph Millar, Gabrielle Calvocoressi, Destiny Hemphill, Marlanda Dekine, Eduardo C. Corral, and Meta DuEwa Jones. Thank you to Cousin Lisa D. Hayes for your research and love of the family. Thank you to the Cave Canem Foundation for providing a space to make these poems sing. Thank you to Copper Canyon Press and editor Ashley E. Wynter for your wisdom and guidance.

De Lissa Daye, who helped me search for the language of Black spaces, thank you for your honesty and support and for asking the difficult questions about my work.

To the people of Nassau Street, you have given me such an important craft.

About the Author

Tyree Daye was raised in Youngsville, North Carolina. He is the author of the previous poetry collections *Cardinal* (Copper Canyon Press, 2020) and *River Hymns* (American Poetry Review, 2017), winner of the APR/Honickman First Book Prize. A Cave Canem Fellow and a Palm Beach Poetry Festival Langston Hughes Fellow, Daye is also a Whiting Award recipient, a Kate Tufts Discovery Award finalist, and a 2021 Paterson Poetry Prize finalist. He was the 2019 Diana and Simon Raab Writer-in-Residence at the University of California, Santa Barbara, and received an Amy Clampitt Residency. Daye is an assistant professor at the University of North Carolina at Chapel Hill. In January 2023, Daye served as guest editor of the Academy of American Poets Poem-a-Day series.

Poetry is vital to language and living. Since 1972, Copper Canyon Press has published extraordinary poetry from around the world to engage the imaginations and intellects of readers, writers, booksellers, librarians, teachers, students, and donors.

WE ARE GRATEFUL FOR THE MAJOR SUPPORT PROVIDED BY:

academy of
american poets

OFFICE OF ARTS & CULTURE
SEATTLE

amazon literary
partnership

THE PAUL G. ALLEN
FAMILY FOUNDATION

4
CULTURE

Hawthornden
Foundation

INGRAM
CONTENT GROUP

the point
envision·enact·evolve

Lannan

WASHINGTON STATE
ARTS COMMISSION

ART WORKS.

National
Endowment
for the Arts
arts.gov

The Witter Bynner Foundation
for Poetry

TO LEARN MORE ABOUT UNDERWRITING
COPPER CANYON PRESS TITLES,
PLEASE CALL 360-385-4925 EXT. 103

WE ARE GRATEFUL FOR THE MAJOR SUPPORT PROVIDED BY:

Anonymous

Richard Andrews and
    Colleen Chartier

Jill Baker and Jeffrey Bishop

Anne and Geoffrey Barker

Donna Bellew

Will Blythe

John Branch

Diana Broze

John R. Cahill

Sarah Cavanaugh

Keith Cowan and Linda Walsh

Stephanie Ellis-Smith and
    Douglas Smith

Mimi Gardner Gates

Gull Industries Inc.
    on behalf of William True

Carolyn and Robert Hedin

David and Jane Hibbard

Bruce S. Kahn

Phil Kovacevich and Eric Wechsler

Maureen Lee and Mark Busto

Ellie Mathews and Carl Youngmann
    as The North Press

Larry Mawby and Lois Bahle

Petunia Charitable Fund and
    adviser Elizabeth Hebert

Suzanne Rapp and Mark Hamilton

Adam and Lynn Rauch

Emily and Dan Raymond

Joseph C. Roberts

Cynthia Sears

Kim and Jeff Seely

Tree Swenson

Barbara and Charles Wright

In honor of C.D. Wright,
    from Forrest Gander

Caleb Young as C. Young Creative

The dedicated interns and faithful
    volunteers of Copper Canyon Press